Southern Gospel Music USA

Denis McMillan

www.fallenherofamily.com

First Edition, August 2012

Copyright 2012 © by Denis McMillan

You can order more copies at:

www.fallenherofamily.com

www.deniswayne.com

Dedication to Roger Bennett

Roger Bennett
1959-2007

Roger Bennett (March 10, 1959 - March 17, 2007) was a Southern Gospel pianist, singer, songwriter, and co-founder of the award winning Gospel Quartet Legacy Five. Prior to forming Legacy Five, he served nearly 20 years as pianist for The Cathedrals. Roger will be missed by so many souls that were touched by his sweet spirit and God-given talent around the world. He was the kind of Christian that believed in the power of prayer with results. Back in the 80's our family group opened up a concert for the Cathedrals in Tyler, Texas. The whole group was so encourging to our family, but Roger made us feel really special following the concert. He treated us like equals, even though we were just a local family gospel group. Not too many months later, I was diagnosed with lymphoma cancer. The doctors had given me just a few months to live. Roger received word of my delimma and called me just a few days after the affirmation of my test results. He encouraged me to keep the faith and then prayed that God would heal me. If God doesn't heal today, I wouldn't be writing my eighth book in 2009. Thank God for Christians like my dear friend Roger Bennett, who believed in the Power of Prayer! *dm*

History of Southern Gospel Music

It is speculated that the date of Southern Gospel's establishment as a distinct genre is generally considered to be around 1910. The first professional quartet was formed for the purpose of selling songbooks for the **James D. Vaughan** Music Publishing Company. The style of the music itself had existed for at least 35 years. The existence of the genre prior to 1910 is evident in the work of **Charles Davis Tillman** (1861-1943) who popularized "The Old Time Religion" and "Life's Railway to Heaven." His legacy left him publishing at least 22 songbooks.

Southern Gospel is sometimes called "quartet music" by fans because of the originally all-male, tenor-lead-baritone-bass quartet make-up. Earlier quartets were typically either A cappella or accompanied only by piano or guitar. In some cases a piano and banjo were used. Eventually, additional musicians were added to give a completed sound. Today, a typical modern Southern Gospel group performs with pre-recorded sound tracks augmented by a piano player and possibly a few other musicians. Some of the genre's roots can be found in the publishing work and "normal schools" of Aldine S. Kieffer and Ephraim Ruebush. Southern Gospel was promoted by traveling singing school teachers, quartets and shaped note music publishing companies such as the A. J. Showalter Company (1879) and the familiar Stamps-Baxter Music and Printing Company. Over time, Southern Gospel came to be an eclectic musical form with groups singing black gospel-influenced songs, traditional hymns, A capella (jazz-style singing with no instruments) songs, country gospel, bluegrass and convention songs.

Convention songs typically have contrasting homophonic (A style of composition in which there is one melody and all the voices and accompaniments move rhythmically together. This is opposed to polyphonic, in which each voice may move independently. Homophony is not to be confused with monophony, in which all the voices and accompanying instruments are performing exactly the same notes. In homophony there is a distinct melody with an accompanying harmony, but all move in the same rhythmic pattern) and contrapuntal (Any music that contains two or more voices heard simultaneously.) sections. In the homophonic sections, the four parts sing the same words and rhythms. In the contrapuntal sections, each group member has a unique lyric and rhythm. These songs are called "convention songs" because various conventions were organized across the United States for the purpose of getting together regularly and singing songs in this style. Convention songs were employed by training centers like the Stamps-Baxter School Of Music as a way to teach quartet members how to concentrate on singing their own part. Examples of convention songs include "Heavenly Parade," "I'm Living In Canaan Now," "Give the World a Smile," and "Heaven's Jubilee."

In the first decades of the twentieth century, Southern Gospel drew much of its creative energy from the Holiness movement churches that arose throughout the south. Early gospel artists such as Smith's Sacred Singers, The Speer Family, The Stamps Quartet, The Blackwood Brothers and The Lefevre Trio achieved wide popularity through their recordings and radio performances in the 1920s, 1930s, 1940s and 1950s. On October 20, 1927, The Stamps Quartet recorded its early hit "Give The World A Smile" for Victor, which become the Quartet's theme song. The Stamps Quartet was heard on the radio throughout Texas and the South. Others such as Homer Rodeheaver and the Cathedral Quartet became well-known through their association with popular evangelists such as Billy Sunday and Rex Humbard.

Although still considered primarily "old-timey quartet singing," Southern Gospel was evolving by the 1990s to include more soloists and duos. It was most popular in the Southeast and Southwest, but it had a nationwide audience. The music remained more country than city and more down-home than ostentatious.

In 2005, The Radio Book, a broadcast yearbook published by M Street Publications, reported 285 radio stations in the USA with a primary format designation as "Southern Gospel," including 175 AM stations and 110 FM stations. In fact, "Southern Gospel" was the 9th most popular format for AM stations and the 21st most popular for FM. Southern Gospel radio promoters routinely service more than a thousand radio stations which play at least some Southern Gospel Music each week. Recent years have also seen the advent of a number of internet-only Southern Gospel "radio" stations.

Over the last decade, a newer version of Southern Gospel has grown in popularity. This style is called Progressive Southern Gospel and is characterized by a blend of traditional Southern Gospel, Bluegrass, modern country, contemporary Christian and pop music elements. Progressive Southern Gospel generally features artists who push their voices to produce a sound with an edge to it.

The traditional style Southern Gospel singers employ a more Classical singing style. Lyrically, most Progressive Southern Gospel songs are patterned after traditional Southern Gospel in that they maintain a clear evangelistic and/or testimonial slant.

Southern Gospel purists view lyrical content and the underlying musical style as the key determining factors for applying the Southern Gospel label to a song. Although there are some exceptions, most Southern Gospel songs would not be classified as Praise and Worship. Few Southern Gospel songs are sung "to" God as opposed to "about" God.

On the other hand, Southern Gospel lyrics are rarely vague about the Christian message. This is why our church music leaders should consider the relevance of Southern Gospel Music today. It's rare that you hear a hymn in Church anymore, much less a good ole Southern Gospel Music song! Maybe we should stand up more and let it be known that Southern Gospel Music is still valid in the local church today.

JAMES D. VAUGHAN
1864-1941

James D. Vaughan, the eldest of four sons, was born near Minor Hill, Tennessee in Giles County on December 14, 1864. He was the son of George Washington Vaughan and Mary Eliza Shores Vaughan. His parents had migrated from the North Carolina Piedmont. His father was a Confederate soldier in the Civil War.

James D. Vaughan is considered by most folks to be the father of Southern Gospel Music.

Vaughan grew up in Middle Tennessee surrounded by the sounds of gospel music. As a teenager, he attended his first singing school and showed an early aptitude for shaped note music. By the age of eighteen, Vaughan was teaching singing classes. Shortly thereafter, Vaughan started his first male gospel quartet with his brothers to advertise his school throughout the region. Vaughn launched a music career in Texas after attending a singing school directed by Ephraim T.

Hildebrand, who operated the Hildebrand Burnett Music Company. Hildebrand encouraged Vaughan to try writing his own gospel songs.

By 1896, Vaughan was a published writer in the shaped note gospel collection. A tornado nearly destroyed their small home town in Texas, so they packed up their belongings and moved back to Tennessee. Upon returning to Tennessee, Vaughan began publishing his own music.

In 1900, he published Gospel Chimes which included a collection of shaped note hymns. In 1903, James D. Vaughan Publishing Company was established in Lawrenceburg, Tennessee. In six years, his company averaged sales of sixty thousand songbooks a month.

In 1910, he hired a group of four male singers to travel around the local area and sing in churches and just about anywhere someone would let them perform. Vaughan surmised that having a quartet might be a new avenue to sell his music books. Five thousand songbooks were sold to a crowd of fifteen hundred in the Cumberland Presbyterian Church at their first concert in Tennessee. With this prosperous and successful encounter, he eventually employed sixteen quartets and sponsored trips as far away as Illinois.

Vaughan wrote more than five hundred songs, printed and sold over six million gospel songbooks, founded the first radio station in the state, and pioneered professional Southern Gospel Music.

He died on February 9, 1941, at his home in Lawrenceburg. The community of Lawrenceburg and the southern gospel community remember Vaughan as a pioneer who found his strength in his God.

Downtown Lawrenceburg has honored Vaughan with many memorials, including the Vaughan Memorial Nazarene Church and the James D. Vaughan Museum.

Charlie D. Tillman
1861-1943

Charles D. Tillman was born on March 20, 1861 in Tallassee, Alabama. He was a self educated musician. Reverend Tillman was very active in evangelistic work preaching and singing throughout the nation.

During the World Convention of Christian Workers held in 1893 at Boston, Massachusetts he substituted for Ira Sankey as song leader.

He was a singer, preacher, and lecturer of rare charm. Charlie Tillman engaged in the publishing business issuing twenty different song books. Some of them sold over a quarter million copies. He was also the author and publisher of the "Day School Singer" that was prepared for and adapted for use in the state of Georgia public schools.

He wrote many songs which became widely used and famous such as: "Life's Railway to Heaven", "Old Time Power", "When I Get to the End of the Way", and "The Old Time Religion" Mr. Tillman died on September 2, 1943 in Atlanta, Georgia.

Tribute to the Legendary Blackwood Brothers

The Blackwood Brothers

The name "Blackwood Brothers" is a name that is synonymous with Gospel Music. Their music has been heard around the world on radio, recordings, television and in personal appearances.

The Blackwood Brothers formed in 1934 in Choctaw County, Mississippi. The original members were brothers Doyle Blackwood, James Blackwood, Roy Blackwood and his son, R. W. Blackwood.

In June 1954, the Blackwood Brothers Quartet appeared on the "Arthur Godfrey's Talent Scouts" show on television. They won the competition with their stirring rendition of "The Man Upstairs."

Two weeks after the Arthur Godfrey appearance, two of the Blackwood Brothers, R. W. Blackwood and Bill Lyles were both killed in a plane crash in Clanton, Alabama. The surviving Blackwoods regrouped adding R. W.'s younger brother, Cecil, to sing baritone and J. D. Sumner, singing bass.

In 1956, James Blackwood, Cecil Blackwood and J. D. Sumner organized the first National Quartet Convention which still exists today and is held in Louisville, Kentucky every year in the fall.

The Blackwood Brothers introduced the first customized tour bus. A replica of their bus is on display in the Southern Gospel Music Hall Of Fame at Dollywood there in Pigeon Forge, Tennessee.
Elvis Presley loved gospel music and attended many of the conventions the Blackwood Brothers held at the Ellis Auditorium in Memphis. Backstage, Elvis joined James Blackwood, Hovie Lister and J. D. Sumner for an impromptu rendition of "How Great Thou Art."

When his mother, Gladys Presley, died in 1958, Elvis and Vernon asked the Blackwood Brothers to sing for her funeral. The Blackwood Brothers were touring in North Carolina at the time, however, a plane was chartered and they were able to fly to Memphis. Elvis had them sing many of his favorite songs such as "Rock of Ages," "I Am Redeemed," "Precious Lord Take My Hand," "In the Garden," and his mother's favorite song, "Precious Memories."

The Blackwood Brothers were guests on The Barbara Mandrell Show, Hee-Haw, Tom Snyder, Porter Wagoner, and the Grand Old Opry. They had their own television show for many years. They sang with many great singers such as Johnny Cash, Porter Wagoner, Tennessee Ernie Ford, Jim Nabors, The McGuire Sisters and many more. They also made guest appearances for the Billy Graham Crusades, Liberty Bowl, and the Presidential Prayer Breakfast.

"My first hero was James Blackwood of the Blackwood Brothers Quartet. The first time I heard James Blackwood sing, "I Want To Be More Like Jesus," I just knew somehow from that moment that I wanted to be a singer for the rest of my life. "The music was infectious and inspiring." Larry Gatlin

In the early 80's James joined the Masters V and later formed, "The James Blackwood Quartet." He also continued singing solo at special events. He joined in with several "Gospel Greats" in the concerts and tapings of the Bill Gaither Homecoming Videos.

The Blackwood Brothers have recorded over 200 albums and toured in 47 countries. They've won eight Grammy Awards and six Dove Awards. In 1998, they were honored by being inducted into the "Gospel Music Hall of Fame" in Nashville, Tennessee.

In 2003, we called him "Mr. Gospel Music": The James Blackwood Tribute Album," with The Jordanaires, Larry Ford and The Light Crust Doughboys. We were pleased that it won the Best Southern, Country, or Bluegrass Gospel Album of the Year:

James Blackwood was nominated for a Grammy Award thirty-one different years. The Gospel Music Association has presented Mr. Blackwood with its highest recognition, The Dove Award, seven times for being the top male vocalist in his field.

Southern Gospel Music USA

The Blackwood Brothers

wwwblackwoodbrothers.com

Please note: *This is the web site of Jimmy Blackwood, Billy Blackwood and the Blackwood Brothers Quartet. There are several singing groups that use the Blackwood name. All contacts regarding scheduling of the Blackwood Brothers Quartet are made from our office by Mona Blackwood. We are independent of any other group using the family name.*

1 800-476-7749

By FAX: 901-384-0478

By Mail: PO BOX 280932, MEMPHIS, TN 38168

Ron & R.W. Blackwood Jr. receive "Living Legend Award"

June 14, 2008, Pigeon Forge, Tennessee - To attain legendary status, by definition, one must have accomplished something "remarkable enough to be famous."

According to the Nashville based Music City Gospel Showcase and FAITH magazine, Ron and R.W. Blackwood, Jr. have reached that height. The honor came as a surprise to the brothers, who were waiting backstage at the Grand Convention Center Saturday night. Don and Donna Frost, the father-daughter team at the helm of Music City Gospel Showcase had carefully arranged to surprise Ron and R.W. The two, along with the rest of The Blackwoods were awaiting their introduction to perform when Frost introduced a never-before seen clip of R. W. Blackwood, Sr. singing "I Want to be More Like Jesus." As the beautiful voice of their father filled the auditorium, the Blackwoods were moved to tears.

When Frost announced that the Living Legends Award for 2008 had been awarded to the "second generation of Blackwood Brothers: Ron and R.W., Jr.," with those standing nearby had to literally push Ron on stage to accept the award! Stunned and honored, R.W. and Ron each thanked God for allowing them to do what they love doing, and also graciously thanked the Frosts.

Ron and R.W. Blackwood, Jr. are the sons of Gospel music icon, R W Blackwood; Sr. Their father was one of the founding members of the legendary Blackwood Brothers Quartet.

In 1954, R.W. Blackwood Sr.'s life was taken in a horrible plane crash. Ron and R.W. Jr. were 13 and 11 respectively at the time of the crash.

Ron founded his own rendition of the original group, the "Blackwood Quartet." R.W. Jr. has made his mark on the music industry since the 1960's with the "Blackwood Singers." The two brothers reunited in the Smoky Mountains in 2001 to honor their father and the legacy he left them.

Through the years, members of the Blackwood family have won 8 Grammy Awards, 27 Dove Awards, and 5 All American Music Awards. They have sold millions of recordings worldwide, and have been seen and heard on every major television, radio, and cable media outlets.

The musical legacy of the Blackwood family began before the 1900's and has been carried on for more than a century! The sound took on its signature four-part harmony in 1934, when RW Blackwood, Sr., his father Roy Blackwood, and Roy's brothers Doyle and James founded the original Blackwood Brothers Quartet.

Through the years, the family group has taken on different forms and names, but the legend lives on today through the voices and lives of these talented family members and friends.

Elvis Presley and the "Blackwood Family"

A special bond between Elvis and The Blackwood Family.

Published August 9th, 2005 in News, Press Releases

Pigeon Forge, TN – Elvis Presley certainly made his mark on America. As a matter of fact, he made an American mark on the world, but who influenced Elvis? Every book written about the life of "The King of Rock and Roll" truthfully states that Presley's life was touched by a special, musical family: The Blackwoods.

Ron and R.W. Blackwood, Jr. of The Blackwood Breakfast Variety Show at the Black Bear Jamboree Theater in Pigeon Forge, TN can recall personal memories with Elvis.

"I remember playing football with him. He was very competitive. Elvis said he liked me because I was rowdy and loud. As kids, we were a lot alike." Ron Blackwood

R.W. Blackwood Jr. remembers, *"One day, Ron and I were out throwing a ball in the yard, and we heard motorcycles approaching the house. It was Elvis with Natalie Wood on the back of his motorcycle, and his entourage following. He wanted to show Natalie Wood that he knew The Blackwood Brothers! I'll never forget that!"*

Elvis and The Blackwood family attended church together at the First Assembly of God in Memphis, Tennessee when he was just a poor, dark haired boy in second-hand clothes. Elvis would visit the home of Roy and Susie Blackwood (the grandparents of Ron and R.W., Jr.) for a hot, home cooked meal.

It was RW Blackwood, Sr. (Ron and R.W.'s father) who would let the future super-star into the back door of Blackwood Brothers' concerts in Memphis when the Presley's were too poor to pay the admission price.

In the summer of 1954, Elvis would cry for hours, mourning the loss of his hero and friend, R.W. Blackwood, Sr., in a horrible plane crash. The Blackwood family shares many fond memories of their unique friend.

A discovery upon a recent trip to Graceland served as a reminder of the mutual respect and admiration Elvis held for their music. Located in a display of his favorite recordings was the 1974 Blackwood Singers album called *"A Wonderful Feeling."*

R.W. Blackwood Jr. explains, "We always knew Elvis loved the music of our dad and the Blackwood Brothers, but to find our album…The Blackwood Singers, with the girls and more contemporary music not just in his collection, but ON TOP and on display…that just blew us away!"

www.fallenherofamily.com

www.marktrammellministries.com

Mark Trammell Ministries
PO Box 588
Gadsden, AL 35902

(256) 442-1621

Southern Gospel Music USA

www.thegospelgreats.com

Paul Heil is generally recognized as the best-known radio voice in Southern Gospel Music today. Now into his fifth decade of radio, television and commercial announcing, Paul Heil has been honored with numerous industry awards and fan awards for his work in Southern Gospel Music. His smooth, friendly, thoroughly-professional production style is regularly in demand. He's also been the producer and voice of the popular *Southern Gospel Music Month Daybook* series which was distributed to more than 900 radio stations each September for several years. And he has produced countless special radio features for various record labels which have been distributed to thousands of radio stations.

Indicative of the depth of his involvement in Southern Gospel Music, Paul was a founding member in 1986 of the Southern Gospel Music Guild, a national organization of Southern Gospel Music industry leaders, dedicated to the growth of the music and the resultant spreading of the Gospel. Paul served as president of the Southern Gospel Music Guild longer than anyone else (nine years). He has also served as a vice president of the Gospel Music Association and is a member of the advisory board of the Southern Gospel Music Association (Hall of Fame and Museum).

Paul and his program, *The Gospel Greats*, have won the highest *Singing News* Fan Awards for which they were eligible every year since 1987. The Singing News Fan Awards are generally recognized as the most prestigious fan-voted awards in the Southern Gospel Music industry. And Paul was honored with the Marvin Norcross Award, a prestigious individual award presented by *Singing News* magazine for lifetime accomplishment in the field, in 1991. In 1997, the Southern Gospel Music Guild awarded Paul their "Hearts Aflame" award as "Radio Personality of the Year."

In 2000, *Gospel Voice* magazine named their annual award for radio excellence *"The Paul Heil Award"* and presented it for the year 2000 to its namesake, Paul Heil.

In 2003, Paul was inducted into the Pennsylvania Southern Gospel Music Hall of Fame by the Pennsylvania Southern Gospel Music Association. Heil is a life-long Pennsylvanian and remains a supportive member of the PSGMA.

In 2004, the Southern Gospel Music Association honored Paul with its highest overall award, the **"James D. Vaughan Impact Award,"** *(seen at right)* presented each year to the one individual who has had the greatest lifetime impact on the field of Southern Gospel Music. (The award is named in honor of Vaughan, considered the founder, nearly a century ago, of what has come to be known as Southern Gospel Music.)

In 2007, *SGNScoops Magazine* presented Paul with their highest honor, the "Sharon Smith Impact Award" for outstanding contributions and overall impact on the world of Southern Gospel Music. And voters in thesoutherngospel.com's 2006 Southern Gospel Music Awards voted Paul their "Favorite Radio Personality."

In recognition of his accomplishments, Paul has been selected for biographical representation in *"Who's Who In Religion," "Who's Who In The East," "Who's Who In Entertainment," "Who's Who Among Emerging Leaders in America," "Who's Who In Media and Communications," "Who's Who In The World"* and *"Who's Who In*

America," all respected biographical reference works published by Marquis Publishing, available in most public libraries.

A special version of *The Gospel Greats* program aired for many years (during the late 1980s and early 1990s) around the world on the Armed Forces Radio Network. It was the first Southern Gospel radio program ever accepted for distribution to America's military stationed around the world. An expanded version later aired on the AFTRS FM program service, also a first. Armed Forces Radio personnel presented Paul with a special plaque in honor of his "outstanding support" for America's military personnel stationed around the world through this broadcast. *(Cutbacks in air time allocated to faith-based programming during the Clinton administration ended the program's run there.)*

Today *The Gospel Greats* program airs each week on about 200 radio stations throughout the United States and in Canada. It is also heard around the world on the internet, accessible wherever anyone has a computer and an internet connection. And *The Gospel Greats* was the first nationally syndicated Southern Gospel radio program to be heard on either of the two major satellite broadcasters. It was heard first on Sirius through WSM, Nashville, but later exclusively on XM. Since the Sirius/XM merger, the program now is heard multiple times each weekend on both satellite services — XM's enLighten34channel and Sirius channel 67.

Prior to his present work, Paul was an award-winning radio news director (1969-1977) and a television news director (top 50 market, 1977-1979). During his college years, Paul created and operated a live radio network serving a dozen college radio stations throughout Southeastern Pennsylvania, called the *Keystone Collegiate Radio Network*. In the early 1980s, he syndicated a weekly half-hour public affairs program to more than 60 Pennsylvania radio stations called *Pennsylvania Newsmakers*.

Heil has an earned B.A. in English from Elizabethtown College, Elizabethtown, Pa., and an honorary Doctor of Humanities degree from Emmanuel Baptist University.

Dr. Paul Heil & Dr. William B. Reynolds

Paul Heil, producer and host of *"The Gospel Greats"* syndicated radio program, has been granted an honorary Doctor of Humanities degree by Emmanuel Baptist University of Connelly Springs, North Carolina. **Dr. William B. Reynolds** (above with Paul), president of Emmanuel, conferred the degree during special ceremonies June 16, 2006, at the Pentagon near Washington, DC.

A Special Thanks to Mr. Paul Heil - This author is grateful that Bro. Paul participated in our endeavor to spread the "Good News" throughout this book. We are so blessed to have folks like him, who spend their lives in the good work of our Lord, Jesus Christ. What would we do without Southern Gospel Music? dm

The Legendary "Chuck Wagon Gang Story"

Seventy-two years in any business is a long time, particularly in a musical group of any genre. Today, the Chuck Wagon Gang holds the distinction of being the oldest recording mixed gospel group still performing with ties to the original founding.

By trade, the Carters were farmers, who migrated from place to place to pick cotton. The singing group came from humble beginnings in 1935, as the Carters found themselves in Lubbock, Texas, without enough money to buy medicine for a sick child, Effie. Dave Carter and two of his children, Lola and Ernest of his Carter Quartet (no relation to the Carter Family of Bristol, VA) arrived at radio station KFYO in Lubbock seeking "live" singing employment on radio in order to buy medicine for Effie. They landed the job, Effie soon re-joined them, and the Carter Quartet remained at the station for about a year. The radio response had been so over-whelming that Mr. Carter decided to move his family to Fort Worth, Texas. They auditioned for several stations, and finally hit the big one, 50,000-watt station, WBAP.

Already on the station was a western band known as the Chuck Wagon Gang, sponsored by Bewley Mills. The flour company sent this group out on location advertising the flour, and hot biscuits were served on the spot.

The Carter Quartet was hired by the station and instantly became Bewley's Chuck Wagon Gang. In addition to the group name change, came individual name changes as well for simplicity: D. P. "Dad" Carter (Dave), Anna (Effie), Rose (Lola), and Jim (Ernest). Their repertoire consisted of ballads, folk, western, and popular songs of the day, and one hymn or gospel song each. They became very popular at WBAP, and at one time Bewley Mills offered a picture for coupons from flour sacks. Over 100,000 requests came in to the station.

Two British record producers, Don Law and Art Satherly heard them early on and quickly signed them to an exclusive recording contract with American Record Corporation. Their first recording sessions occurred at a makeshift recording studio at the Gunter Hotel, in San Antonio, Texas on November 25 and 26th, 1936. They recorded twenty-two titles of both gospel and western songs. "The Son Hath Made Me Free" was their first recording. In short time, their gospel recordings became so popular that after three western sessions, the decision was made to only record gospel music.

In short time, the Chuck Wagon Gang's contract and master recordings were purchased by Columbia Records, now Sony Music. Their association with Columbia Records lasted thirty-nine years, during which time they recorded four hundred and eight known masters.

At one time, the Chuck Wagon Gang was the second highest selling artist on the label. The group was quite content with their popular radio program, and on occasion did a few personal appearances in Texas and neighboring states. Their records were being heard nationwide as well as in several foreign countries.

Promoter, the late Wally Fowler heard them on radio, and decided they were a must for his "All-Night Gospel Singings" which were becoming very popular in the South. Traveling to Texas, his mission was to convince the Chuck Wagon Gang that folks outside Texas were ready for live concerts at his programs. The group was very reluctant for these distant travels, but finally booked two dates with him in Augusta and Atlanta, GA. Much to the Gang's surprise, thousands of very enthusiastic folks were on hand to greet them at both cities. The Gang did not know the "norm" for Wally's programs. As a radio group, they sang from songbooks and sung western and gospel songs. They did not even know they were to sing all gospel music at Wally's programs and have the lyrics memorized like other gospel groups.

Much to the surprise of other groups on the program, they sang from their songbooks at these two engagements. In short, the Gang did not like all the traveling associated with concert appearances. Unfortunately, most of Wally's programs were in the Eastern United States, but they granted him several 10-day sporadic tours during the early years. Except for brief interruptions during World War II, their radio shows lasted 15 years, but their career was mounting for full concert work.

Eventually, their travels would take them to the famed Carnegie Hall in New York City, Hollywood Bowl, Gator Bowl, and Daytona International Speedway along with numerous appearances on The Grand Ole Opry. They also traveled internationally to Canada, Nassau and the Spanish Wells in The Bahamas.

The Gang's popularity was greatly enhanced by radio play. One could hardly move the radio dial without hearing them. Many locally sponsored 15-30 minute daily radio programs, playing only Chuck Wagon Gang music, sprouted across the nation. In the 1950's, promoters Rev. and Mrs. J. Bazzel Mull of Knoxville, TN began playing their music exclusively weekly on large 50,000-watt stations in Nashville, Chicago, New Orleans, and other large cities.

Millions of records and songbooks were sold across the nation as well as many foreign countries from the Mulls' radio shows. Around 1956, the group briefly moved headquarters from Texas to Knoxville, and Rev. Mull became their booking agent.

Turning to television in the early 60's, they made a number of black and white video clips for The Wally Fowler Show and The Mull's Singing Convention. The Chuck Wagon Gang also co-hosted a TV Show with The Rangers Trio, The Gospel Roundup, a fifteen-minute Monday-Friday show, featuring two songs by each group. This program was aired and rerun for approximately five years. They made numerous guest appearances on several of the popular country music shows including The Wilburn Brothers and Porter Wagoner.

As with any organization and particularly a music group, personnel changes were inevitable and expected for various reasons. The Chuck Wagon Gang remained essentially a family group through the years. As family members retired or left the group, other family members as well as non-family members came into the group. To date, forty-eight known individuals have played their respective roles in the Chuck Wagon Gang. This is not a lot of people, considering the longevity of the group. Each addition to the group has remained a close-harmony quartet and contributed to the onward success of the considered, "legendary" Chuck Wagon Gang.

Through the years, many awards and accolades have been bestowed upon the group. The first commercially licensed recording of the now Albert E. Brumley classic; "I'll Fly Away" was the Chuck Wagon Gang's recording of the title on December 16, 1948. In 1950, Billboard reported that disc jockeys of America voted the Chuck Wagon Gang eighteenth most popular of all small singing groups in the nation, considering all genres of music and third most popular of all Columbia Recording artists.

Anna Gordon was awarded "Miss Gospel Singer" in 1954. In 1955 Columbia Records awarded them their first gold record for "I'll Shout and Shine," commemorating 20 years on Columbia Records.

Also in 1955, the National Disc Jockey Associated voted them "Number One Gospel Act in America." They were named the "Kentucky Colonels in the mid-sixties.

In 1966, The Chuck Wagon Gang was chosen with several other artists to appear in a movie, "Sing a Song for Heaven's Sake."
Columbia Records also presented a 30-year plaque in 1967.

Dad Carter was posthumously inducted into the Gospel Music Association's Hall Of Fame in Nashville on April 3, 1985.

On November 28, 1986, performance rights organization SESAC presented the Gang's second gold record "to commemorate 50 years of recorded music, an unparalleled milestone in Gospel Music."

"The Lifetime Achievement Award" was awarded in 1986 by SESAC.

The 50th anniversary also included a letter from President Ronald Reagan. The States of Texas and Tennessee also bestowed special honors.

In 1989 Rose Karnes was presented "The Living Legend Award" by The Grand Ole Gospel Reunion, followed by her sister, Anna, received the same award in 1990.

In 1989, at the National Quartet Convention in Nashville, Roy Carter was presented the coveted "Marvin Norcross Award," the highest honor given in the gospel music field. The Chuck Wagon Gang garnered "Gospel Group of The Year" by TNN/Music City News Awards for the years 1988, 1989, 1991, 1992, and 1993.

The group was nominated for a Grammy Award in 1992 for their album, "Still Rollin," placing in the top five of their category.

In 1998 all past and former members of the 'Gang' were inducted into the Gospel Music Association's Hall of Fame in Nashville, TN.

In 2006, Shaye Smith was made a "Kentucky Colonel." On June 14, 2006, President Bush sent White House greetings in honor of the Chuck Wagon Gang's 70th Anniversary.

In October 2005, Anna Carter Gordon Davis was inducted into the Southern Gospel Music Association's Hall of Fame in Pigeon Forge, TN. Anna was followed by her sister, Rose Carter Karnes for the same induction in October 2006.

Their recordings are among the historic recordings at both the White House and The Smithsonian Institute in Washington, DC.

www.fallenherofamily.com

The Chuck Wagon Gang

www.thechuckwagongang.net

SHAYE SMITH
MGR
The Chuck Wagon Gang
PO Box 140416
Nashville, TN 37214-0416

817-944-2538
704-472-0060

Southern Gospel Music USA

www.theparishfamilymusic.com

The Parish Family
P.O. Box 7054
Bainbridge, GA 39818

229-861-2917

www.fallenherofamily.com

www.southernsoundquartet.com

Southern Sound Quartet Ministries, Inc
6340 Spera Point Crossing
Nashville, Tn 37076

615-883-7375
615-481-9431

Southern Gospel Music USA

The Pfeifers
120 W. Court Street Suite 4
Washington Court House, OH 43160

740-335-9641

Beckie Simmons Agency

615-595-7500

www.fallenherofamily.com

www.theascensionqt.com

The Ascenscion Quartet
Danny Parnell
17202 Hwy 64
Lebanon, MO 65536

(417) 533-7883

(417) 860-7444 (cell)

32

www.karenpeckandnewriver.com

The Harper Agency
P.O. Box 144
Goodlettsville, TN 37070

615-851-4500
Fax: 615-851-9461

www.fallenherofamily.com

Down East Boys

www.downeastboys.com

Dominion Agency

Michael Davis
PO Box 1277
Waynesville, NC 28786

828–454–5900

Southern Gospel Music USA

www.perrysministries.com

The Harper Agency
P.O. Box 144
Goodlettsville, TN 37070

615-851-4500
Fax: 615-851-9461

www.fallenherofamily.com

www.diplomatsqt.com

The Diplomats
3185 East Hwy. 166
Carrollton, GA 30116

770-832-2930

The McKameys

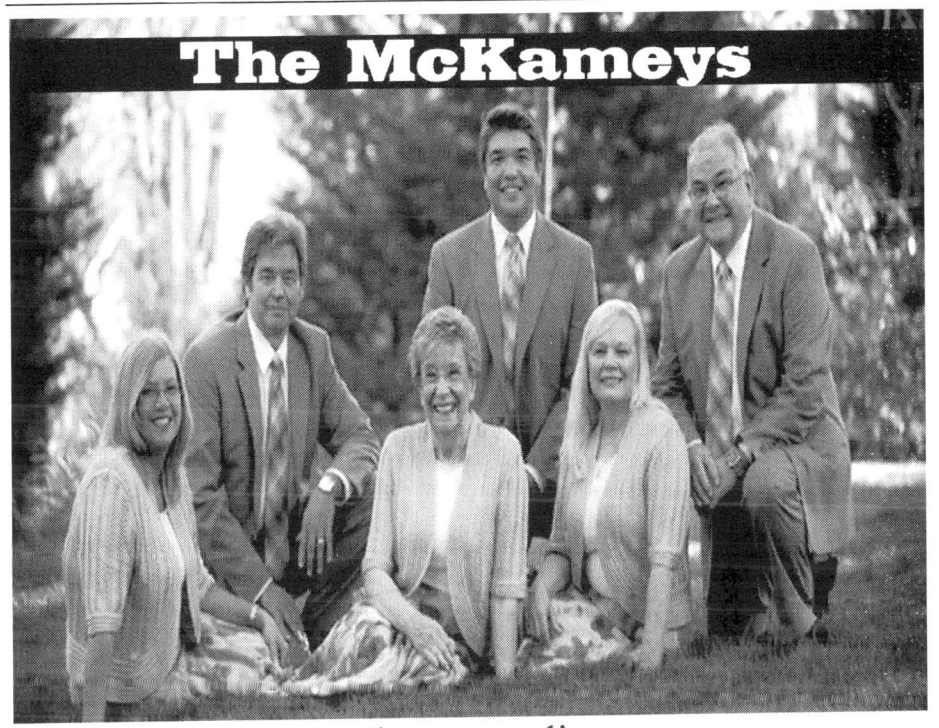

www.mckameysonline.com

**The McKameys
PO Box 128
Clinton, Tn 37717**

**The Harper Agency
P.O. Box 144
Goodlettsville, TN 37070**

**615-851-4500
Fax: 615-851-9461**

www.fallenherofamily.com

www.dixieechoes.com

**Dixie Echoes
481 Ronda Street
Pensacola, Florida 32534
Phone: (850) 477-6391**

**Rivergate Talent Agency
Post Office Box 312
Hermitage, TN 37076
(615) 649-8181**

Southern Gospel Music USA

www.tpq4him.com

The Proclaimers Quartet
6121 Gateway Road
Columbus, Georgia 31909

706.561.6062

www.fallenherofamily.com

Tribute to the Florida Boys

Consistency, class, dignity, stability, and reliability immediately come to mind when describing the "Florida Boys." No quartet in the history of gospel music has better represented these adjectives. There is no other professional group in the history of gospel music that has spent more consecutive years on the road without a hiatus than the Florida Boys. The Florida Boys have exemplified the best in gospel music for more than fifty years.

Jessie Gillis (JG) Whitfield loved to sing gospel music. He had sung gospel music prior to his service in the Air Force during World War II. When he returned from the service, he joined with Roy Howard, Edward Singletary, "Tiny" Merrill, and Guy Dodd to form the Gospel Melody Quartet. Whitfield was able to financially under gird the quartet due to his success in the retail market. The popularity of the quartet kept growing through the south until the voice of lead singer, Roy Howard, was stilled when he had a fatal heart attack. The quartet continued to sing with several vocalists filling the various positions in the quartet. Doyle Wiggins finally settled in as lead singer for the quartet and Whitfield hired Glen Allred as baritone and guitarist. Glen had just left the Oak Ridge Quartet and was an invaluable addition to the Gospel Melody Quartet. Soon, the military called Doyle Wiggins and Les Beasley was offered the position as lead singer for the quartet. Les had just left the military service himself. The group with Buddy Mears (tenor), Les Beasley (lead), Glen Allred (baritone), JG Whitfield (bass), and Livy Freeman (pianist) began to appear quite frequently on the major quartet concerts in the southern United States.

Wally Fowler was one of the top gospel music promoters of the day, and he used the Gospel Melody Quartet quite frequently. Whenever the Gospel Melody Quartet would perform on one of Fowler's programs, he introduced them as "The boys from Florida with sand in their shoes and a song in their heart!" It quickly became apparent that the group was better known by this moniker instead of the rather nondescript sounding name of the "Gospel Melody Quartet." At Fowler's suggestion, Whitfield abruptly changed their name to "The Florida Boys" in the mid 1950s. With the support of Wally Fowler and the promotional prowess of JG Whitfield, the Florida Boys continued upon a career that would surpass almost every group in the gospel music industry. Several popular gospel artists were in the group in the 50s including George Younce and Tommy Fairchild as bass singer and baritone singer respectively. Derrell Stewart joined the group as pianist in 1956 and remains on their piano bench some fifty years later. Although his hairstyle has changed periodically, his red socks have been his trademark throughout his hall of fame career.

JG Whitfield had experienced grief in his life in the early 1950s with the tragic death of his wife, Ruth. He married the former Hazel Sturgis in 1958 and it soon became apparent that family life was more important to Whitfield than the life of a road warrior. He resigned his position as bass singer in the quartet, yet remained a vital part of the group both as promoter and friend.

After Whit's retirement from the road, Les Beasley took over the helm as manager of the quartet . . . a position he still holds nearly fifty years later. Les is known throughout gospel music as the finest quartet manager in the business. The Florida Boys thrived under Les and his watchful eye.

Billy Todd replaced JG Whitfield as bass singer in the Florida Boys. Todd was another service veteran, and had also been a winner on Arthur Godfrey's Talent Scouts. His talent wasn't his singing but rather his instrumental imitations . . . a talent he also brought to the stage with the Florida Boys.

The Florida Boys became well known through their regional television program, "The Gospel Song Shop" which was produced by JG Whitfield. Whitfield also was the emcee for the program and spokesman for the sponsor, Black Draught Laxative and Solstice Rub. How appropriate that a gospel program would be sponsored by a laxative! They were included as headliners on the first gospel music concert held in Carnegie Hall. The Florida Boys were advertised on this program as the most televised gospel quartet in the nation. This exposure led the Florida Boys to their role as headliner for the new gospel music television program, "The Gospel Singing Jubilee."

Les Beasley was the producer of the Gospel Singing Jubilee. The Gospel Singing Jubilee became the best known and longest running television program in the history of gospel music. The popularity of the Florida Boys increased exponentially as they appeared in the living rooms of gospel music fans throughout the country each Sunday morning. Many of us remember getting ready for church as we listened to the musical strains of "Jubilee, Jubilee . . . you're invited to this happy jubilee!" The original Jubilee crew consisted of the Florida Boys, the Couriers, the Happy Goodman Family, and the Dixie Echoes. Les was responsible for bringing some of the biggest names in gospel music onto the set of the Jubilee. It was always a thrill awaiting the guest groups as they would come over the hill singing "JUBILEE!"

Each program would begin with the Florida Boys singing their latest songs to a national audience. The popularity of the Florida Boys continued to grow as did the viewers of the Gospel Singing Jubilee. During this time, the Florida Boys often appeared in concert with "Little" Steve Sanders. This pairing helped to expand the audience of the quartet to a younger genre.

The quartet released several records on the "WHIT" label prior to their first recording on the Skylite record label. The quartet did several recordings on the Songs of Faith label in the early 1960s. The Florida Boys was the first group signed to the Canaan record label. Canaan Records was a subsidiary of the Word record company designed to spotlight traditional gospel quartets. "The Florida Boys in Nashville" was one of the first albums released on this label in 1965. Their affiliation with Canaan Records lasted for well over a decade and a half.

The personnel of the Florida Boys remained unchanged for several years. Coy Cook left the Florida Boys in 1967 to join JG Whitfield and his Dixie Echoes. The Florida Boys hired Tommy Atwood to replace Cook. Atwood was quite a different singer than Cook, for he had a background in bluegrass music. He was also quite proficient on the fiddle (otherwise known as the violin for you classical music folks!) With Atwood singing tenor, the quartet embraced a more "country" sound than in previous years. Bluegrass inspired instrumentals featuring Atwood on the fiddle and Allred on guitar became a highlight of a Florida Boys concert.

Tommy Atwood remained with the Florida Boys for several years and became quite beloved by the fans of the quartet. In the early 1970s, Tommy left the group to explore other ministry opportunities. Billy Todd retired from the quartet soon thereafter. However, the nucleus of Beasley, Allred, and Stewart remained intact as did the sound of the Florida Boys.

Laddie Cain, a former member of the Plainsmen, assumed the tenor position for several years. In keeping with the consistency of the quartet, Buddy Liles replaced Billy Todd and remained with the quartet for more than two decades. Buddy was also a quartet veteran having sung with groups including the Orrell Quartet, Rhythm Masters, Landmark Quartet, and Rebels Quartet.

The quartet continued to have many successful songs during the ensuing years. Songs such as "Standing on the Solid Rock," and "When He Was on the Cross, I Was on His Mind" continued to keep the Florida Boys at the top of the gospel music charts.

Four of the quartet positions remained intact for many years, yet the tenor position was a virtual revolving door. As many quartet managers will lament, the tenor spot is tough to retain. After Laddie Cain left the Florida Boys, Jerry Trammell (brother of Mark Trammell) joined the quartet for several years. Through the years, quite a few others have filled the tenor slot for the Florida Boys including in no particular order Paul Adkins, Johnny Cook, Mark Flaker, Don Thomas, Terry Davis, Rick Busby, Greg Cook, and Billy Hodges. Must be something about the surname "Cook" and Florida Boys tenors!

The Florida Boys finally settled on a young music major, Allen Cox to fill the tenor position. Allen occupied that spot with the quartet for several years. Shortly after Allen joined the quartet, Buddy Liles retired after many years of service to the Florida Boys. Gene McDonald was hired to sing bass with the quartet. This infusion of youth into the quartet seemed to revitalize the Florida Boys. Gene and

Allen brought wonderful musical ideas to the quartet. Allen's background in musical theater and Gene's gospel music experiences opened new doors for the quartet.

Les Beasley has always been known as an innovator in gospel music. In addition to his work with the Florida Boys, he's also well known as a television producer and a fixture with the National Quartet Convention. He's responsible for naming the "Dove Awards." There is little that has happened in gospel music in the last 40 years that hasn't had Mr. Beasley's stamp of approval. With all these accolades, the one that stands out in my mind is his unselfishness. He understood that the Florida Boys had great potential, but in order for this potential to be fully realized, a change was inevitable. Several years ago, Les relinquished his longstanding position as lead singer with the Florida Boys to newcomer Josh Garner. This unselfish act of humility has propelled the Florida Boys into the upper echelon of traditional quartets of today. The quality of the music the quartet has since tackled has been second to none in gospel music today. Their recent acapella project has demonstrated a prowess that few in the gospel music industry could even attempt to recreate.

The latest personnel change for the quartet again involves the tenor position. Allen Cox recently resigned from the quartet in order to spend more time with his wife and new child. The quartet couldn't have made a better choice to fill their tenor position. Harold Reed, formerly of the Dixie Melody Boys, now sings tenor with the Florida Boys. His voice and stage presence fits the Florida Boys perfectly.

The current group of Florida Boys has it all. They can sing an old convention song with the same confidence as they do an acapella number. Josh Garner is one of the finest up and coming lead singers in gospel music today. His effortless techniques and endless range add credibility to that assessment. Gene McDonald has one of the most pleasing bass voices in gospel music, yet his range far surpasses that of the normal bass singer. Harold Reed continues to impress both old and new fans of the quartet with his wonderful tenor voice. Little can be said about the three SGMA Hall of Fame members of the Florida Boys that hasn't been said before. Derrell Stewart, Glen Allred, and Les

Beasley are three of the most influential artists ever to take the gospel music stage. Time has been kind to the members of the Florida Boys. Tommy Atwood and Billy Todd continue to perform with the other members at the Grand Ole Gospel Reunion. Coy Cook passed away several years ago, but I'm not aware of any other former Florida Boys taking their place in the Heavenly choir. Many have made humorous comments about the Florida Boys and their "loud" stage outfits. I must say that there are few active quartets that I admire or respect more than the Florida Boys. Any group that boasts three SGMA Hall of Famers has my utmost respect. It has been my pleasure to enjoy this great quartet for more than 40 years, and I hope to continue to do so for many more years. Les, Glen, Derrell, Gene, Josh, and Harold, you have my respect both as friends and as artists. May you have another 50 great years in gospel music!

Article posted for the 2005 Grand Ole Gospel Reunion

www.fallenherofamily.com

The Florida Boys

thefloridaboys.net

864-421-3889

1910 · SOUTHERN GOSPEL MUSIC · 2010
100th Anniversary
James D. Vaughan

Southern Gospel Music USA

www.spoken4qt.com

**Spoken 4 Quartet
One Summit Drive
Kimberling City, Mo.
65686**

417-230-3637

www.fallenherofamily.com

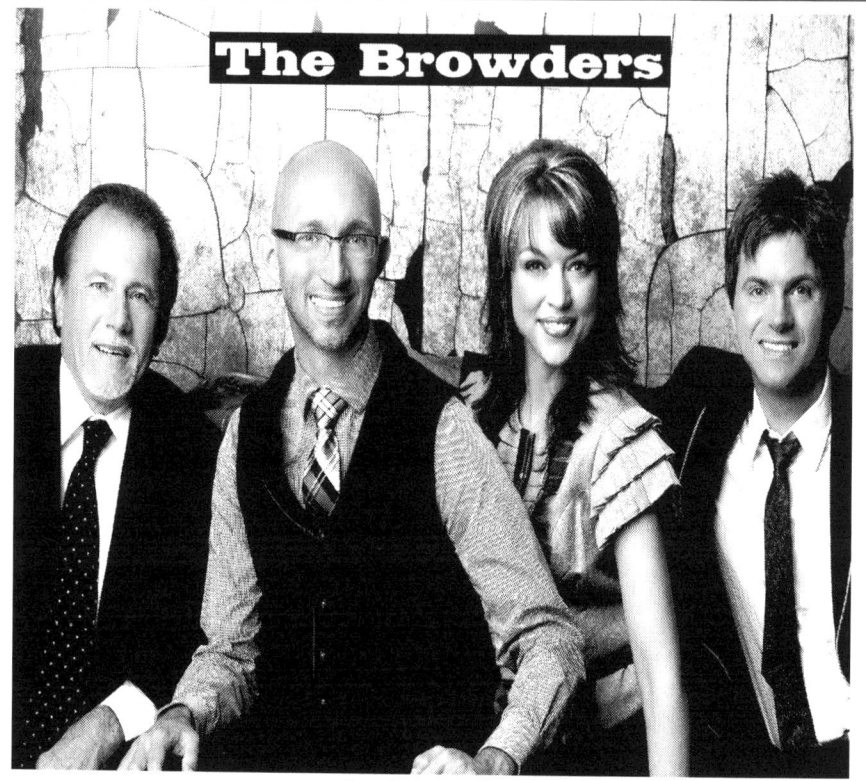

www.thebrowders.com

The Browders
180 Zinc Mine Drive
Hiltons, VA 24258

Booking--423-863-5264
Office--276-225-0421

The Hemphills

www.thehemphills.com

**Joel & LaBreeska Hemphill
P.O. Box 656
Joelton, TN 37080-0656**

(615) 299-0848

(615) 299-0849 (Office Fax)

www.fallenherofamily.com

Rom. 1:16
We Sing The Gospel

Reggie & Bridgette
Saddler
Family

www.saddlerfamily.com

Reggie Saddler
5323 Bill Sain Rd,
Vale, NC 28168

704-276-1374

Southern Gospel Music USA

The Dove Brothers

www.dovebrothersquartet.com

The Dove Brothers Quartet
15605 Highway 131
Bladenboro, North Carolina 28320

910-640-9025

Fax: 910-863-3161

www.fallenherofamily.com

Danny Funderburk

www.dannyfunderburkministries.com

**Danny Funderburk Ministries
P.O. BOX 335
Indian Trail, NC 28079**

704-441-5853

Southern Gospel Music USA

www.triumphantquartet.com

**Dominion Agency
P.O. Box 1277
Waynesville, NC
28786**

828-454-5900

www.fallenherofamily.com

www.theinspirations.com

**The Inspirations
P. O. Box 1338
Bryson City, NC
28713**

828.497.2060

www.brianfreeandassurance.com

The Harper Agency
P.O. Box 144
Goodletsville, Tennessee
37070

615-851-4500

www.fallenherofamily.com

www.whisnants.com

**The Whisnants
2824 NC 126
Morganton, NC 28655

828.584.4118 day
828.584.1502 evening
828.584.3176 fax**

www.theballbrothers.com

The Ball Brothers
79 Liberty Dr.
Chickamauga, GA 30707

501-317-9833

www.fallenherofamily.com

TheHarperFamilyMusic.com

The Harper Family
P.O. Box 53
Bunker, Mo 63629

(573)247-4374

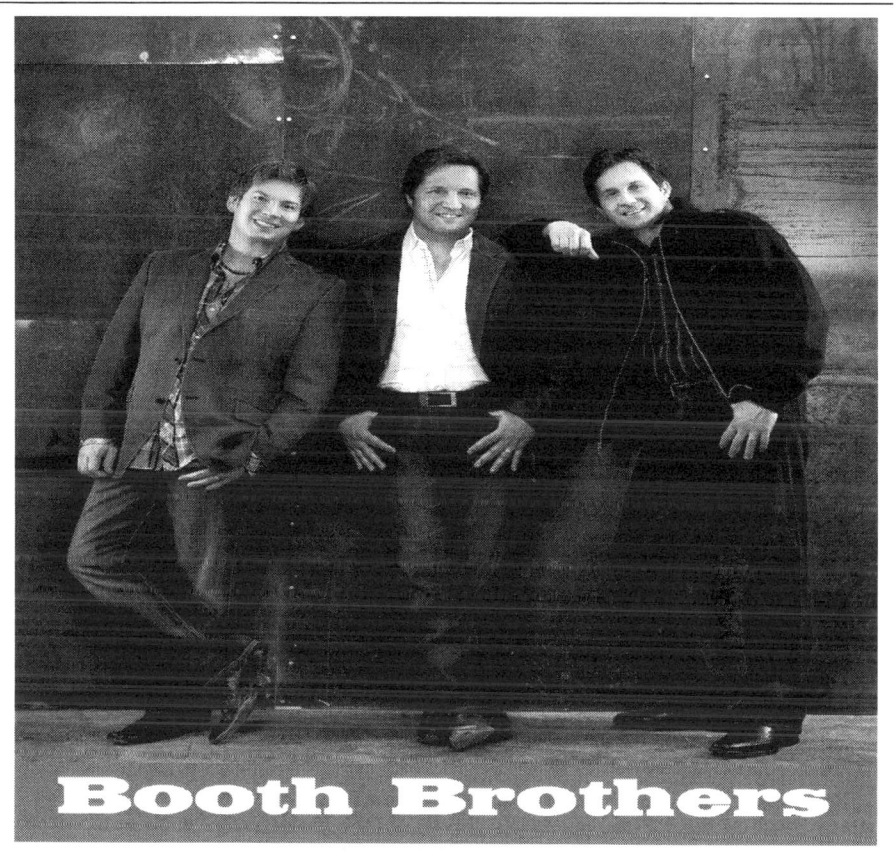

www.boothbrothers.com

The Booth Brothers
PO Box 847
Spring Hill, TN 37174

1-866-722-6884

www.fallenherofamily.com

www.the-freemans.com

**The Freemans
P.O. Box 2514
Hendersonville, TN
37075-2514**

Fax: **(615) 824-7570**

(615) 824-6161

Southern Gospel Music USA

www.legacyfive.com

The Harper Agency
PO Box 144
Goodlettsville, TN 37070

(615) 851-4500

www.fallenherofamily.com

www.psqworld.com

**The Beckie Simmons Agency
5543 Edmonson Pike #10
Nashville, TN. 37211**

615-595-7500

www.thetaylorsmusic.com

The Taylors
P.O. Box 2252
Lillington, NC 27546

910- 528-6522

www.fallenherofamily.com

The Collingsworth Family

www.thecollingsworthfamily.com

Danette Haddix, Office Manager

P&KC Music
P.O. Box 158
New Richmond, OH 45157

513-553-0658

Southern Gospel Music USA

Crimson Gold

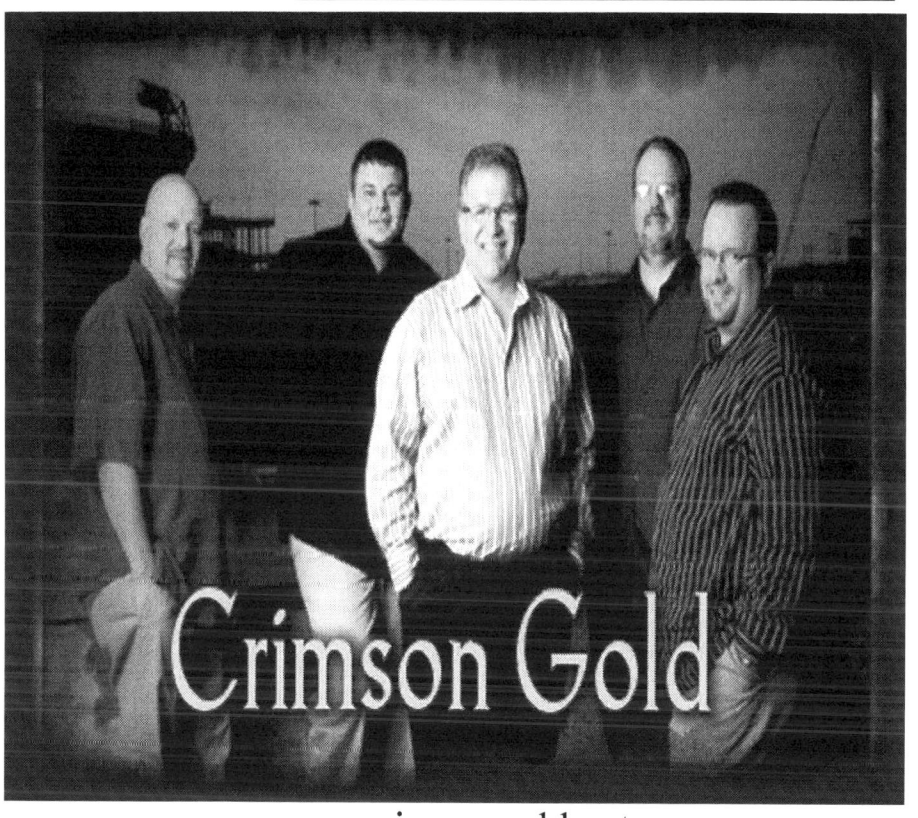

www.crimsongold.net

Kent Mathes
573-734-1269

Ray Reese
573-637-2121

www.fallenherofamily.com

www.forgiven-quartet.com

Forgiven Quartet
4848 Melody Lane
Bartlesville, OK 74006

918-850-6446

thebrownsmusic.com

**The Browns
116 Central Ave.
LeMars, IA 51031**

888-202-2712

thebrownsmusic@aol.com

Southern Gospel Radio:

Yesterday, Today, Tomorrow

Paul Heil wrote the following feature article for *Singing News* magazine, which appeared in their May, 2007, issue (pages 82-83).

Radio broadcasting in America first appeared in the early 1920s, at least in a form that we would recognize as broadcasting. And since at least 1922, what we call Southern Gospel Music has had a continuous and beneficial relationship with radio.

1922 was the year **James D. Vaughan**, the man often referred to as the founder of Southern Gospel Music, founded WOAN radio in Lawrenceburg, Tennessee. His music of choice? Southern Gospel quartets, of course. His goal was to promote his singing school and his songbooks. It worked. People heard the music and loved it. And radio made it possible.

In fact, in those early years, publishers such as Vaughan and the Stamps-Baxter Music Company regarded radio exposure for their music as essential. The late James Blackwood once told me that such broadcasts were "really putting Southern Gospel Music on the map." The **Blackwood Brothers**, of course, were very popular on the radio, heard on many stations nationwide via transcription (special broadcast records). Blackwood told me their agency once estimated, based on the amount of mail their broadcasts received, that they had "a million people listening to you everyday on the radio." And, indeed, Blackwood Brothers records promoted on their broadcasts sold in huge numbers, far beyond anything in the field today.

Back then, into the 1940s and 50s, especially, most "professional" quartets had such programs. They would do a live broadcast in the morning, promote their concert (within driving distance), and then have their concert that night. **Glen Payne** and **Hovie Lister** (an early Gospel DJ) were others who loved to tell me stories about the early days in radio and the impact it had as it introduced more and more people to their quartet singing. It was the primary means to promote the music.

Key to Survival

I don't think it's far-fetched to say that radio is, in a natural sense, what has allowed Southern Gospel Music to survive and thrive over the past eighty-some years. Radio has been the primary "connection" between the artists (and their record companies) and fans at large. It's how most people first find out about Southern Gospel Music. It's where most fans first hear new songs. Radio has been an obvious means of promoting group concert appearances. Radio produces the charts that influence which artists promoters book. Radio creates a demand for recordings, thereby helping support the "industry," including, of course, the artists. And radio has inspired generations of singers to become a part of the field. Most of the artists I interview, in fact, cite radio as an early influence in their love for Southern Gospel singing.

One of those singers was a young fella from Indiana, **Bill Gaither**. Milking cows early in the morning, the barn radio would deliver the **Statesmen** or other top quartets of the day. "As a kid twelve years old, not caring much what they were singing, it was just fun, fun music for me and they got my attention," Gaither recalls. "After they got my attention, I started listening to the lyric, and I said to myself, 'this is serious stuff,' and I literally found Christ through the radio. So that's the reason the radio was so important to me." *(Talk about an impact!)*

Modern Radio Experiences

And there is an example of the most important impact Southern Gospel Music can have on radio — changing lives through the message in the music. And that's just as true today as ever.

"What's most interesting is the way the Holy Spirit moves on the listeners during a song set," says **Kyle Dowden**, program director at **KWFC-FM**, Springfield, MO. "As a DJ, I might not have put much thought into the song selection, but I realize God is at work when the phone starts ringing with folks crying, because what was just aired touched them in a unique way... I believe this music is filling people with hope in a difficult world."

Sandi Milam at **WJLS**, Beckley, WV, shares this account: "I had a listener call and talk to me about the new song from the Whisnants, 'A Greater Yes.' The listener said that they had been praying about a particular situation and were wondering why God hadn't answered. When they heard that song they realized that God had something greater in mind for them. It was the answer they needed."

Mildred Drake at **WDFB**, Danville, KY, says many listeners have been saved as a result of their music. "Some new converts said they had so many questions and every question was answered either through a song or message they heard on WDFB."

Phil Cross wrote a song called *"On The Radio"* to illustrate the importance of radio to people. "The first place I focused in that song," Cross says, "was in a rest home and a precious lady of God who can't travel outside her room. She lives on a lonely street. And her connection with the world is through radio. Her whole world is that radio station. And being able to listen to Gospel music and hear somebody sing 'Amazing Grace' — that's her world."

Listener Testimonies

My files are full of listener testimonies about the impact of Southern Gospel Music on the radio. One man, a police officer, would listen to *The Gospel Greats* program while on patrol. "During that time those words [in the songs you played] began to minister to me and the Holy Spirit began to deal with me and began to bring me back to the place where He wanted me to be... It was through your program and through the words, especially of the Cathedrals, and the song that they did, 'Boundless Love.' The ministry that the words of that song did in my life began to put me on a track that led back to the Lord. I began to search and search and I got back into church and I got back into the Scriptures." That man has since entered the ministry.

A Louisiana listener wrote, "I was going through some trying times in my life. Satan was fighting me and trying to beat me down... **Gold City** has a song, *'I'm Not Giving Up.'* That song inspired me and helped me to stay focused on Christ. When you aired that on one of your shows back in July, I got a blessing..."

This Alabama listener expressed perhaps the most common sentiment we hear along these lines: "Many, many times the exact message I needed to hear from God has been delivered to me through your program." This has to be a "God thing" because no amount of "programming savvy" could consistently accomplish that.

One young West Virginia listener recently wrote, "I listen almost every week and I enjoy it thoroughly and so do my mom and dad. I've been struggling with my music for a long time and when I listened the first time I decided that I don't need the world's music anymore."

Words such as those are music to any Southern Gospel broadcaster's ears. And that's really what makes Southern Gospel Music on the radio special. It's music that can impact lives for Christ.

What about The Future?

But, now in its ninth decade on the radio, can Southern Gospel Music continue to have such an impact?

"Yes," say broadcasters we've polled. But it won't happen on its own. "We need to keep our standards of broadcasting high," says **Jon Lands** of **WVVW**, Parkersburg, WV. "There is no room for sloppiness and wasted airtime... Furthermore, we are representing the Lord Jesus Christ as an ambassador in the world of radio. It is imperative that we be the best ambassador possible."

Rich Bruce of **WTRM**, Winchester, VA, says what's needed is "keeping one's on-air presentation intimate (one-to-one), local, professional and Christ-centered." After all, he says, "Southern Gospel radio reflects more than just someone's taste in music; it reflects and reinforces a lifestyle."

Dowden, of **KWFC**, notes, "The music put out by today's top artists is of very good quality, from the writing to the singing to the production. It is having a much greater impact today on those that listen, and will continue that impact as long as there is someone wanting to hear the music."

Radio, in its traditional form and in its newer satellite and online forms, has been, is, and will continue to be the lifeline for Southern Gospel Music, so long as the music itself remains of high quality, solid, encouraging and uplifting — and focused on the Gospel.

Southern Gospel music's #1 radio program with Paul Heil — The Gospel Greats
Heard on great radio stations coast-to-coast!

Paul Heil's *THE GOSPEL GREATS* radio program is the best-known and most widely-respected syndicated Southern Gospel Music radio program, presently airing on more than 200 great radio stations across America, in Canada, on XM and Sirius satellite and on the internet worldwide each week (through affiliates and on-demand).

BAY AREA GOSPEL MUSIC ASSOCIATION

BAGMA
PO Box 262428
Houston, TX 77207-2428

713.641.5529
Fax: 713.641.6944

www.fallenherofamily.com

www.gospelexpress.org

**Gospel Express
1500 Toll Road
Chappell Hill, Tx
77426**

(877) 836-7400

Southern Gospel Music USA

The Gospel Messengers

www.thegospelmessengers.org

For Booking Information

Call 281-383-2286

www.fallenherofamily.com

www.heartsofgracemusic.com

PO BOX 1918
BRAZORIA, TEXAS 77422

979.798.5024

**FOUR STATES GMA
PO BOX 1127
TEXARKANA, AR 75504-1127**

www.4statesgma.com

www.fallenherofamily.com

The Hendrix Trio

www.thehendrixtrio.com

Texarkana, Texas

903-792-3011

Humble Hands Quartet

www.humblehands.net

Paul Petty
ptpdad@embarqmail.com

903 895 2309
903 987 9281

www.fallenherofamily.com

Masterpeace Quartet

www.masterpeacequartet.com

T.L.R. Agency
Tracie
masterpeacequartet@yahoo.com

903-278-1257

www.oneaccordgospel.com

OneAccord
c/o Linda Rhodes
5529 Lakeside Drive
Bossier City, LA 71111

318-549-9454

www.fallenherofamily.com

LeFebre Quartet

www.thelefebrequartet.com

770-967-0400
info@lefevrequartet.com

The Beckie Simmons Agency

www.bsaworld.com

615-595-7500

www.trustinghymn.com

**Trusting Hymn
1104 N. Munson
Roysc City, Texas 75189**

972-636-2316

www.fallenherofamily.com

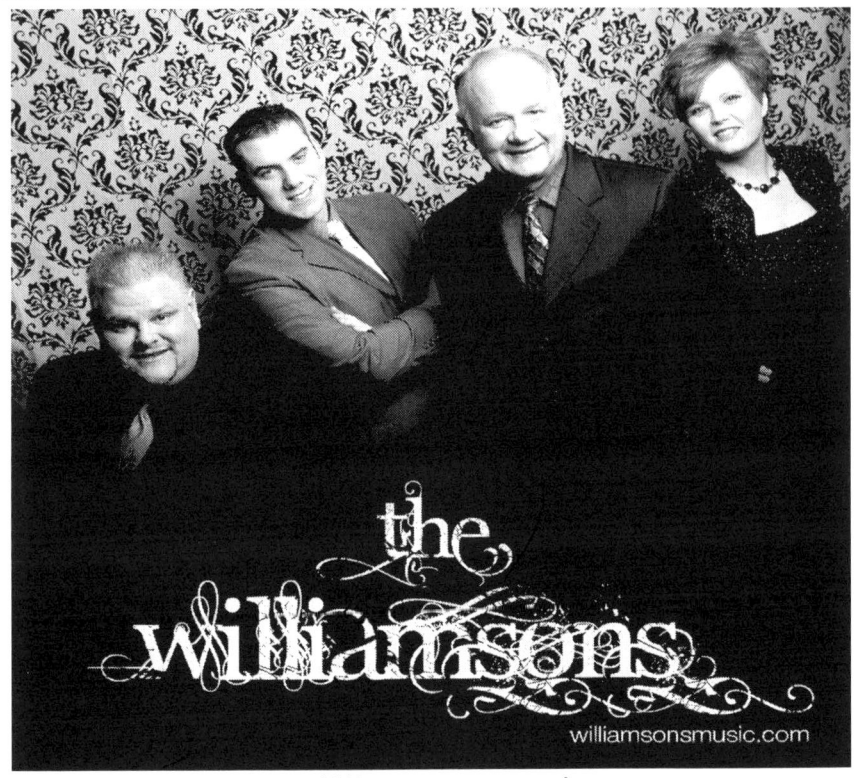

www.williamsonsmusic.com

booking@williamsonsmusic.com

405-380-2761

**Gospel Music Artists Association
PO Box 8903
Greenville, TX 75404**

www.thegmaa.com

www.fallenherofamily.com

www.makeajoyfulsound.com

**Joyful Sound
5025 Coral Creek
Fort Worth, TX 76135

817-781-1683**

www.heavensound.com/artists/masterstouch.htm

Master's Touch
3630 Forest Trail Dr.
Grand Prairie, TX 75052

214--499-5698

The Gospel Station Network
P O Box 1343
Ada, Oklahoma USA
74821

580-332-0902 (business office)
800-557-8815 (toll-free in the USA)
580-332-0922 (fax line)

email@thegospelstation.com

"It's more than just music; it's the gospel of Jesus Christ!"

www.thegospelstation.com

Southern Gospel Music USA

The Chancellors Quartet

www.chancellorsquartet.com

800-558-6475

www.fallenherofamily.com

HEAVEN'S CALL

www.heavenscallministries.com

Heaven's Call
P.O. Box 211
Palos Heights, IL 60463

630.816.4281

www.themarshallsmusic.com

The Marshalls
412 Jordan Drive
Anamosa, Iowa 52205

319.462.3136
319.373.3180

www.fallenherofamily.com

www.theheritagequartet.com

**The Heritage Quartet
7804 Van Wyck Rd.
Lancaster, SC 29720**

**803-285-1087
888-803-6060**

www.reflectionofgracemusic4him.com

Group Mailing Address
67 Small Creek Lane
Hendersonville, NC 28792

(828) 329-3831
(828) 674-5464

www.fallenherofamily.com

Vessels of Praise

www.vopministry2000.com

**Vessels of Praise
18 Bradshaw Lane
Laurens, SC 29360

864-684-5409**

Ken Clubb Singers

www.kenclubbsingers.com

**Ken Clubb Singers
3214 Hilldale Road
West Columbia, SC 29170**

803-796-0682

www.fallenherofamily.com

Gabriel's Call

www.gabrielscall.com

**(803) 760-2699 - Russell
(706) 564-3715 – Ron**

gabrielscall1@aol.com

Southern Gospel Music USA

Master's Praise

www.masterspraise.com

314-575-8117

Master's Praise
acappella vocal group

www.fallenherofamily.com

www.reliablechevy.com

THE BIG LOT
AT RELIABLE CHEVROLET

3655 S. Campbell
Springfield, Missouri
65807

1-866-760-0682

Special Thanks to the Big Lot at Reliable Chevrolet for their support of Southern Gospel Music & The Families of our Fallen Heroes!

Chevy Runs Deep

Joy Evangelistic Association

JEA, (Joy Evangelistic Association) is a non-profit Christian organization 501-C3 in Springfield, Mo. that began back in 1993. The sole purpose of the organization is to give financial relief to those in crisis that include missions, pro-life organizations, evangelistic ministries, handicapped children, cancer groups and legitimate community needs.

JEA also contributes to the "Freedom Alliance" and the "Wounded Warriors Project" who support the families of our fallen heroes.

When you purchase this book, a generous portion of the proceeds are contributed to these wonderful non-profit organizations. *Dm*

Heaven Yes, Hell No!

Denis McMillan

www.fallenherofamily.com

Made in the USA
Charleston, SC
04 February 2013